Famous Myths and Legends of the World

Myths and Legends of North America:

CANADA AND NORTHERN UNITED STATES

WORLD BOOK

a Scott Fetzer company
Chicago
www.worldbook.com

World Book, Inc.
233 North Michigan Avenue
Suite 2000
Chicago, Illinois 60601 U.S.A.

For information about other World Book publications, visit our website at www.worldbook.com or call 1-800-967-5325.

Library of Congress Cataloging-in-Publication Data

Myths and legends of North America: Canada and Northern United States.
      pages cm. -- (Famous myths and legends of the world)
   Summary: "Myths and legends from Canada and the Northern United States. Features include information about the history and culture behind the myths, pronunciations, lists of deities, word glossary, further information, and index"-- Provided by publisher.
   Includes index.
   ISBN 978-0-7166-2626-8
   1. Indian mythology--North America--Juvenile literature.
   2. Indians of North America--Religion--Juvenile literature.
   3. Indians of North America--Folklore--Juvenile literature.
   I. World Book, Inc. II. Series: Famous myths and legends of the world.
   E98.R3O37 2015
   398.2089'97--dc23
                              2015014765

Set ISBN: 978-0-7166-2625-1

Printed in China by PrintWORKS Global Services,
Shenzhen, Guangdong
1st printing July 2015

Writer: Cynthia O'Brien

Staff for World Book, Inc.
Executive Committee
President: Jim O'Rourke
Vice President and Editor in Chief: Paul A. Kobasa
Vice President, Finance: Donald D. Keller
Director, International Sales: Kristin Norell

Editorial
Manager, Annuals/Series Nonfiction: Christine Sullivan
Managing Editor, Annuals/Series Nonfiction:
   Barbara Mayes
Administrative Assistant: Ethel Matthews
Manager, Indexing Services: David Pofelski
Manager, Contracts & Compliance
   (Rights & Permissions): Loranne K. Shields

Manufacturing/Production
Director: Carma Fazio
Manufacturing Manager: Sandra Johnson
Production/Technology Manager: Anne Fritzinger
Proofreader: Nathalie Strassheim

Graphics and Design
Art Director: Tom Evans
Coordinator, Design Development and Production:
   Brenda Tropinski
Senior Designers: Matthew Carrington,
   Isaiah W. Sheppard, Jr.
Media Researcher: Jeff Heimsath
Manager, Cartographic Services: Wayne K. Pichler
Senior Cartographer: John M. Rejba

Staff for Brown Bear Books Ltd
Managing Editor: Tim Cooke
Editorial Director: Lindsey Lowe
Children's Publisher: Anne O'Daly
Design Manager: Keith Davis
Designer: Kristine Hatch
Picture Manager: Sophie Mortimer

CONTENTS

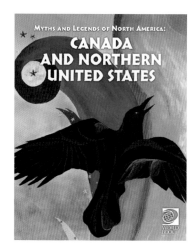

The raven is one of the first birds mentioned in mythology and appears in the myths of many peoples. In many North American myths, Raven is the victim of tricks played by Coyote.

Raven Releasing the Sun, Moon, and Stars (1996), detail from mural by Jennifer Headtke; Seward Mural Society, Seward, AK (© Walter Bibikow, Danita Delimont Stock Photography/Alamy Images)

Note to Readers:

   Phonetic pronunciations have been inserted into the myths and legends in this volume to make reading the stories easier and to give the reader some of the flavor of the Canadian and Northern United States cultures the stories represent. See page 64 for a pronunciation key.

   The myths and legends retold in this volume are written in a creative way to provide an engaging reading experience and approximate the artistry of the originals. Many of these stories were not written down but were recited by storytellers from generation to generation. Even when some of the stories came to be written down, they likely did not feature phonetic pronunciations for challenging names and words! We hope the inclusion of this material will improve rather than distract from your experience of the stories.

   Some of the figures mentioned in the myths and legends in this volume are described on page 60 in the section "Deities of Canada and Northern United States." In addition, some unusual words in the text are defined in the Glossary on page 62.

INTRODUCTION

Since the earliest times, people have told stories to try to explain the world in which they lived. These stories are known as myths. Myths try to answer these kinds of questions: How was the world created? Who were the first people? Where did the animals come from? Why does the sun rise and set? Why is the land devastated by storms or drought? Today, people often rely on science to answer many of these questions. But in earlier times—and in some parts of the world today—people explained natural events using stories about gods, goddesses, spirits of nature, and heroes.

Myths are different from folk tales and legends. Folk tales are fictional stories about animals or human beings. Most of these tales are not set in any particular time or place, and they begin and end in a certain way. For example, many English folk tales begin with the phrase "Once upon a time" and end with "They lived happily ever after." Legends are set in the real world, in the present or the historical past. Legends distort the truth, but they are based on real people or events.

Myths, in contrast, typically tell of events that have taken place in the remote past. Unlike legends, myths have also played—and often continue to play—an important role in

The World of the Crow People, page 52

a society's religious life. Although legends may have religious themes, most are not religious in nature. The people of a society may tell folk tales and legends for amusement, without believing them. But they usually consider their myths sacred and completely true.

Most myths concern *divinities* (divine beings). These divinities have powers far greater than those of any human being. At the same time, however, many gods, goddesses, and heroes of mythology have human characteristics. They are guided by such emotions as love and jealousy, and they may experience birth and death. A number of mythological figures even look like human beings. In many cases, the human qualities of the divinities reflect a society's ideals. Good gods and goddesses have the qualities a society admires, and evil ones have the qualities it dislikes. In myths, the actions of these divinities influence the world of humans for better or for worse.

The World of the Arapaho, page 40

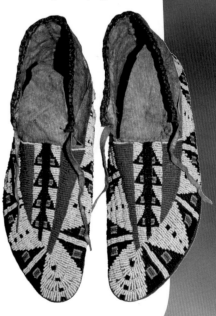

Myths can sometimes seem very strange. They sometimes seem to take place in a world that is both like our world and unlike it. Time can go backward and forward, so it is sometimes difficult to tell in what order events happen. People may be dead and alive at the same time.

Myths were originally passed down from generation to generation by word of mouth. Partly for this reason, there are often different versions of the same story.

The myths in this volume come from the cultures of Native Americans who lived throughout what are now Canada and the northern United States, from the Arctic to the central Plains and from the Atlantic to the Pacific coasts.

In early times, every society developed its own myths, though many myths across cultures share similar themes, such as a battle between good and evil. The myths of a society generally reflect the landscape, climate, and society in which the storytellers lived.

Myths of Canada and Northern United States

To Native American culture, myths are as important as food or shelter. Although Native American religions differed by tribe and region, a belief in a mysterious force in nature was widespread. The Indians told many myths about this spirit power, which they considered superior to human beings and capable of influencing their lives. People depended on the unseen spirit for success in the search for food and in healing the sick, as well as for victory in war. Some tribes believed in a great spirit—an especially powerful god. But the great god belief was always accompanied by a belief in many other spirits or in the general spirit power.

According to Native American belief, the unseen spirit might be centered in some animals, areas, or things, making them powerful or dangerous. Thus, living in harmony with the natural world was essential.

The North American landscape provided the settings for Native American myths. People of the Eastern Woodlands, who were farmers and villagers, told stories that related to their lives around the Great Lakes, for example. The Western nations of the Great Plains were hunters. Their myths often related to buffalo hunting and a nomadic life. The sky stretched for miles over the plains, so many myths took place in the sky or were about the sky. In the north, the Arctic people relied on the sea for survival. The sea and its creatures were essential to the stories that they told.

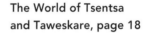

The World of Tsentsa and Taweskare, page 18

By studying myths, we can learn how different societies have answered basic questions about the world and the individual's place in it. We can learn how a people developed a particular social system with its many customs and ways of life. By examining myths, we can better understand the feelings and values that bind members of society into one group. We can compare the myths of various cultures to discover how these cultures differ and how they resemble one another. We can also study myths to try to understand why people behave as they do.

KWATEE

and the Animals

This story from the people of the Northwest Coast explains how a powerful being created the animals of Earth and the people who rely on them.

The Time of Beginnings was different from the world we know today. Humans did not yet exist, and Earth was controlled by the giant animal people. Kwatee (KWAHT ee), the Changer, did not like what he saw. He wanted to use his powers to make Earth a better place. He made the rivers flow, and he filled the rivers with fish. Kwatee wanted the world to be ready for the people who

The giant animal people grew angry with Kwatee. They did not want any changes made to Earth. As Kwatee traveled and made his changes, the giant animal people tried to trick him. But Kwatee was too clever for them. The giant animal people did not know that Kwatee could disguise himself. They did not recognize him because he changed his appearance so many times.

One day, Kwatee, the Changer, who was in disguise, came upon one of the giant animal people. The animal man told Kwatee that he was making a knife to kill the Changer. Kwatee said that the knife would make a fine weapon and asked to see it. When the giant animal man handed it over, Kwatee plunged the knife between the animal man's ears and told him that he would now be a deer. Kwatee did this so the deer would provide food for the people to come.

Next, Kwatee came across a giant animal man making a club. Again, he tricked the animal man into giving him the weapon. Then Kwatee struck the animal man on his back. Kwatee told him that he would now be a beaver. The beaver would flap its tail and live in the river. It would eat trees. Its fur would provide warm clothing for the people to come.

After some time, Kwatee had changed all the giant animal people into the animals we know today. When he was finished, he took sweat from his body and mixed it with soil to make mud, which he rolled into balls. From these balls of mud and sweat, he made the first people. He made other people from dogs. After he created all the people, Kwatee taught them to make tools from stones. With Kwatee's help, the people grew healthy and strong. They had many children and were happy.

Later, Kwatee faced another difficult challenge. It came in the shape of a huge monster that lived beneath the waters of a lake. One day, Kwatee's brother was canoeing on the lake when the beast rose up from the water and swallowed him. Kwatee was enraged to lose his brother. He threw red-hot rocks into the lake. The water boiled and burned the monster so that it died. Kwatee then slit the monster's body open and released his brother.

Eventually, Kwatee grew old. He was greatly pleased with all the changes he had made in the world. He sat down on a rock and looked over the ocean. After he watched the sun set, Kwatee pulled a blanket over his head and turned into stone.

The World of KWATEE

The Native Americans of the Pacific Northwest told this story to explain the creation of two important animals in the people's lives—deer and beaver. The tribes of the region included the Suquamish (suh KWAH mish), the Duwamish (duh WAH mihsh), the Snoqualmie (SNOH kwahl mee), and the Muckleshoot (MUHK uhl shoot). These peoples spoke versions of the same language, Salish (SAY lihsh), and shared many myths and stories.

Native Americans in canoes arrive at the Seattle waterfront for the Salmon Homecoming Celebration. The festival honors the fall return of salmon to the rivers of the Pacific Northwest as well as Native American culture.

THE BEAVER

Many beavers lived in the rivers and lakes of the Pacific Northwest. Native peoples in North America trapped beaver and used their fur to make clothes. After Europeans arrived in North America from the 1500's onward, there was a great demand for furs to export to Europe. In the late 1800's, the expanding fur trade reached the north Pacific coast. Beavers were in high demand. European hatmakers used beaver hair to make felt hats. Trappers traded with native hunters for beaver pelts, but some groups, including the Nez Perce (nehz PURS), refused to hunt for or trade beavers with the Europeans.

A felt hat made from beaver fur

Whidbey Island is one of many islands in Puget Sound, a system of connected inlets and bays on the west coast of Washington State. Carved by glaciers, the sound is a mix of waterways, islands, and wetlands. Most of the sound's shores are high and wooded. The sound is about 100 miles (160 kilometers) long and about 10 miles (16 kilometers) wide. Today, Puget Sound is a leading American shipping center. The ports of Seattle, Tacoma, Bremerton, Olympia, and Everett stand on its banks.

GIANT ANIMALS

Giant animals occur in myths told by many different Native American peoples. These animals usually have great powers or strength. The Haudenosaunee (hoe dee noh SHOH nee) have the Great Bear, a creature that eats humans. The Plains and Northwest Coast people honored the giant Thunderbird. Thunderbird was a helpful creature who protected the people from evil forces— which included another giant animal, the Great Owl Woman, who, the people believed, brought the harsh winter.

The great blue heron is one of many animals attracted to Puget Sound by the easy availability of food. Other animals that make their home in the sound include salmon, bald eagles, harbor seals, orcas, sea lions, and humpback whales.

THE DUELING BROTHERS

The nations of the Haudenosaunee (hoh dee noh SHOH nee) Confederation tell the story of twin brothers to explain why the world is both wonderful and dangerous.

Long, long ago, Sky Woman gave birth to a daughter. The daughter grew into a beautiful young woman. One day, the young woman went for a walk. She walked west without knowing why. The West Wind noticed her beauty and swept her up. Sky Woman's daughter soon felt the West Wind's children come to life inside her. When the time came, she gave birth to twin boys, Taweskare (tah weh skah reh) and Tsentsa.

As soon as the boys were born, their mother died. The boys' grandmother, Sky Woman, was heartbroken. She buried her daughter in the earth.

Immediately, green shoots grew from the soil. The plants grew taller and became corn, beans, and squash. Then tobacco grew from the daughter's heart and strawberries from her feet. Sky Woman's daughter became Mother Earth to all the people.

Sky Woman took care of her grandsons, who could not have been more different. The twins grew into strong young men, but they argued all the time. Sky Woman sighed, but she could not stop them. During one angry fight, their grandmother tried to step between them, but they were so mad at each other that

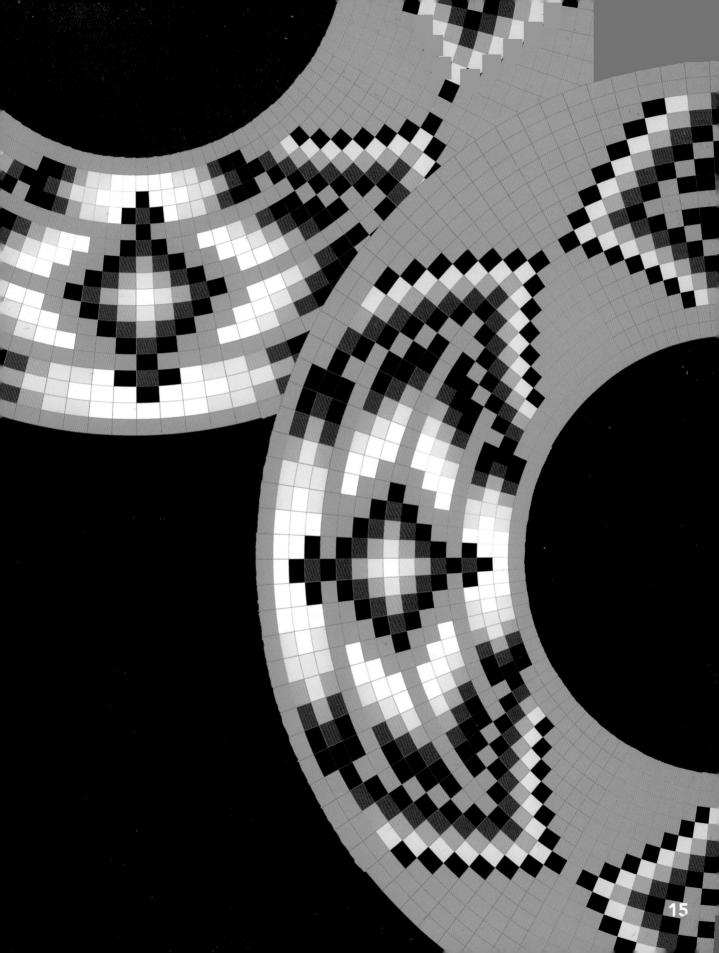

they did not stop fighting. Accidentally, they killed Sky Woman and ripped off her head. The brothers threw the head into the sky, where it became the moon.

After seeing what they had done, the twins finally stopped fighting. Like their grandmother and mother, the twins had powers—but each had a different plan. Tsentsa, the noble twin, used his powers to make the Sun to balance the Grandmother Moon. Next, Tsentsa created tall, strong trees and wide plains. Then he made such gentle animals as the deer and rabbit. Seeing his brother create these wonderful creations made Taweskare, the other twin, angry. As soon as he could, Taweskare put knots in the tree trunks and created poisonous plants. Then he made treacherous mountains and cliffs. He created dangerous snakes and wolves to attack the gentle animals.

Tsentsa continued to make Earth better for people. He created sparkling streams and winding rivers. But Taweskare continued to damage Tsentsa's work. He threw jagged rocks into the streams. He created rapids so the rivers were dangerous to cross.

Finally, Tsentsa thought the world was ready. He created people from red clay

He blessed the people and protected them with his goodness. Tsentsa warned his brother to stop releasing his evil on the world. But Taweskare refused to change his ways. So Tsentsa challenged his brother to a duel. Whoever won the duel would have power over the world.

The brothers battled for many days. Eventually, Tsentsa overpowered his twin. He banished Taweskare far to the west. In his angry rage, Taweskare made the volcanoes and hot springs that still erupt in the west today.

The World of
TSENTSA AND TAWESKARE

The Haudenosaunee (how dehn oh SHOH nee) are also known as the Iroquois (IHR uh kwoy). In the early 1600's, these Native Americans formed a federation of tribes that once occupied most of what is now New York state in the northeastern United States. The tribes included the Mohawk (MOH hawk), Oneida (oh NY duh), Onondaga (ON uhn DAW guh), Cayuga (kay YOO guh), and Seneca (SEHN uh kuh). The Iroquois Federation was the most efficient North American Indian organization. The confederation of states that became the United States of America may have been patterned after the league.

A LAND OF EXTREMES

According to the myth of the Dueling Brothers, Taweskare (tah weh skah reh) was responsible for many of nature's difficulties. Long, cold winters that lasted for months meant the people could not farm all year long. Bears and wolves were threats to both the people and the animals they hunted, including deer. However, the good creations of Tsentsa meant that the land was fertile for farming during the growing season, and the many trees provided wood for longhouses and canoes.

The Haudenosaunee were farmers as well as hunters. They depended on corn, which, according to myth, grew from the body of Sky Mother's daughter, the mother of the dueling twins.

The name *Haudenosaunee* means *we longhouse builders.* Longhouses were large, rectangular buildings made of tree bark in which a number of families lived.

Modern Native Americans perform traditional dancing at the Kanatsiohareke Mohawk Indian Festival in New York state. The Mohawk make up one of the tribes of the Haudenosaunee Confederation. In addition to New York state, the Mohawk live in the Canadian provinces of Ontario and Quebec.

GOOD vs. EVIL

The fight between the twins is a fight between good and evil. A similar struggle is central to many myths around the world. In Egyptian mythology, an evil serpent from the underworld attacks Ra, the good sun god. In the mythology of India, the god Vishnu restores the balance between good and evil by fighting back the evil demons. In many myths, good usually overcomes evil.

The Haudenosaunee saw wolves as threatening creatures that had been created by the evil twin, Taweskare.

In winter, the lands of the Haudenosaunee were often covered in snow, and life became more difficult.

Many peoples of the North American woodlands told stories about deer, which provided food and hides as well as antlers for tools.

COYOTE

Creates the Nez Perce

The Nez Perce (nehz PURS) told this myth to explain why they were different from their neighbors, the Blackfeet and the Crows, though all three tribes came from the body of a monster.

In the time before people, Great Monster ruled the land. Great Monster was so large that he filled a deep, wide valley. He did not have to move to find food because he could breathe in animals from miles away. He ate all of the animals from near and far. He ate the rocks and the plants, too. He opened his giant mouth and swallowed them whole.

As Coyote, the Trickster, listened to tales of the monster, he grew angry. He knew he must save his friends. Coyote asked the Great Spirit for guidance. The

Great Spirit gave Coyote courage and wisdom to go ahead.

Coyote climbed over the mountains to reach Great Monster. When he could see the monster's enormous head, he hid in the grass. He covered himself in clay to disguise his body, then collected two flint stones. He sharpened one of the stones into a knife, hid the knife in his mouth, and called to Great Monster.

Coyote teased Great Monster from the long grass. He shouted out that he could swallow the monster. To show how he might do this, Coyote took a loud, deep breath, but of course, he could not swallow the monster. Finally, Coyote challenged the monster to try to swallow him.

Immediately, Great Monster sucked in Coyote and swallowed him whole. Coyote fell down, down inside the monster. When he came to Great Monster's heart, he took out his flint stone. He used the flint to make a fire that burned through the monster's eyes and ears. Then Coyote cut into the monster's heart with his knife, and the great beast died right away. As Great Monster died, its mouth gaped wide open. Its eyes and ears opened, too. Coyote and the other animals swallowed by the monster ran from the openings, overjoyed to be free.

Coyote cut up Great Monster's body. He threw the pieces to the sunset, the sunrise, the warm land, and the cold land. All these pieces became the people of those lands. The Blackfeet people came from Great Monster's feet. The Crow people came from his

Then Coyote took some water from the river to wash the blood from his hands. He sprinkled the blood and water around the land where he stood. These drops became the Nez Perce (nehz PURS) people. Coyote told the Nez Perce that they would be small in numbers but that

The World of COYOTE

The Nez Perce (nehz PURS) originally lived in the region where the borders of what are now the states of Idaho, Oregon, and Washington meet in the northwestern United States. Prospectors overran the Nez Perce reservation after discovering gold there in the 1860's. Today, the tribe lives in north-central Idaho.

Boys of a Nez Perce tribe prepare for a horse race.

LAND OF MOUNTAINS AND RIVERS

The rugged landscape of the Northwest Coast is central to the myths of the Nez Perce culture. The snow-capped mountains and rolling foothills of such ranges as the Cascades surrounded them. (That may be why the monster in "Coyote Creates the Nez Perce" lives in a deep valley.) The Snake River (right), which flows through Nez Perce territory, was an abundant source of salmon and other fish.

A mound in the Kamiah (KAM ee eye) Valley called "The Heart" is said to mark the spot where Coyote killed Great Monster, who had swallowed all the animals. According to myth, the monster once filled the entire valley.

COYOTE THE TRICKSTER

Many cultures tell stories of a trickster. Tricksters often take the form of an animal, such as the coyote. Tricksters represent uncertainty. They are not trustworthy, even though they sometimes act heroically. Sometimes they help people, but at other times they cause mischief. In this Nez Perce myth, Coyote is a hero. He tricks Great Monster and rescues the animals on which the people depend for food. He also creates the Nez Perce people and their neighbors.

SEDNA THE SEA GODDESS

The Inuit (IHN yu iht) of the far north tell this myth to explain why the waters of the northeastern Pacific Ocean and Arctic Sea provide abundant food but are sometimes dangerous.

A Inuit girl called Sedna (SEHD nuh) lived with her family in a small village. She was happy to live at home. Her father was a good hunter, so Sedna had plenty to eat and warm furs to wear. As she grew older, Sedna became more and more beautiful.

When Sedna reached the age when most young women married, many men in her village asked her to be their wife. Sedna refused all of them. She told her father that she did not wish to be anyone's wife. Her father was worried. He told Sedna that she must marry a good husband who would take care of her, because that was the usual way of things. Sedna's father reminded her that one day he would not be there to feed and clothe her, and that she would need a husband to do those things. Even so, Sedna continued to refuse to marry any of the men who proposed to her.

One day, a handsome stranger arrived in the village. Sedna had never seen anyone like him. The stranger asked Sedna to be his wife. He promised her that he would provide a good home for her. He said she would never be hungry if she went away with him. Sedna thought he would make a much better husband than any of the village men. Her father was happy that she was finally going to marry. So Sedna married the stranger and left the village with him.

Sedna and her new husband traveled across the sea to an island. As their boat neared the island, Sedna could not believe her eyes. Her husband's home was a nest! It was nothing but moss and sticks. How could she live in such a place? Then, suddenly, her husband changed from a handsome man into a bird. The bird had tricked Sedna. He could not bring Sedna meat and furs. He could only catch fish!

The bird forced Sedna to live in the nest and eat the fish he caught. Sedna was extremely unhappy. She was hungry for meat, and she missed her comfortable home. She hated her bird husband. She cried every day for her father to come and rescue her.

The wind carried Sedna's cries to her father. He got in his kayak and paddled across the sea. Sedna was overjoyed to see him. Quickly, she got into the kayak. Sedna and her father hurriedly paddled away from the bird's island before the bird could return from fishing. But the bird returned early. Furious to see his wife leaving, he flew across the sea and chased Sedna and her father. Sedna's father hit the bird's wings with his paddle. That made the bird even angrier. He flapped his wings and a terrible storm began.

The winds blew, and waves crashed against the sides of the kayak. Sedna and her father became frightened. They tried desperately to hang on as the kayak rolled from side to side. Sedna's father grew frantic. He had to find a way to stop the storm, or they would both drown. He knew that the bird was angry that Sedna had run away, so he decided to offer his daughter as a sacrifice to the sea gods.

In a flash, Sedna's father threw her overboard. Desperately, Sedna tried to hold on to the kayak. Sedna's father thought the storm would stop only if Sedna drowned. So he cut off her fingers with his paddle. As the fingers fell into the ocean, they became seals.

Still Sedna tried to hold onto the edge of the boat with all that was left of her hands. Again, her father tried to beat her off with his sharp paddle. Sedna's hands, too, fell into the icy water. They became whales.

Finally, Sedna let go. She fell to the bottom of the sea. At once, the sea became calm and the storm ended.

As she lay on the seabed, Sedna changed. She became the Goddess of the Sea. Since that time, people have never known how the Sea Goddess will behave. Sometimes, Sedna is kind. She allows the sea to provide animals for the people. However, when Sedna is angry, she makes the sea angry, too. Then she keeps the animals from the people and causes great storms instead.

The World of SEDNA

The Inuit (IHN yu iht) live in and near the Arctic, farther north than any other people in the world. Their homeland stretches from the northeastern tip of Russia across Alaska and northern Canada to Greenland. The Inuit were skilled hunters who depended on the abundant sea life of the region for food, including harp and harbor seals, orca, and beluga whales. The traditional way of life has ended for most Inuit. Many Inuit now live in towns, but hunting and fishing are still part of Arctic life.

Baby harp seal

The Inuit live in one of the coldest and harshest regions of the world. Most kinds of plants and animals cannot live as far north as the Inuit do. Their Arctic landscape includes tall mountains and featureless plains. Pack ice floats on the ocean, and glaciers cover vast areas. The ground stays frozen, even in the summer. But during the summer, the sun does not set for months, so the weather is warmer and people enjoy the light all night long. Their traditional clothing, made from sealskin and furs, is warm and waterproof.

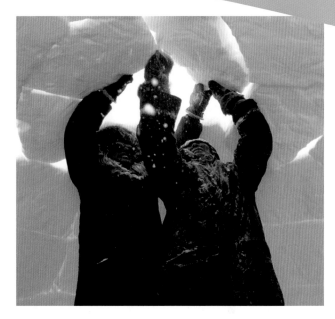

Modern Inuit use blocks of snow to construct an igloo. *Igloo* is the Inuit name for a shelter. Traditional Inuit shelters were made of snow, sod, or stone. The best-known igloo is the dome-shaped winter snowhouse of the Canadian Inuit.

An Inuit mask of a mother and child is made of caribou hide and trimmed in fox fur. Caribou-hide masks are a recently developed art form among First Nations people of Canada. Traditionally, the Inuit carved masks from wood or bone. The masks are usually worn for religious ceremonies and dancing.

FAMILIES

Unlike many other First Nations bands, the Inuit did not have chiefs. Traditionally, Inuit culture was based on the family rather than on a tribe. In Inuit society, the father was the head of the family and was responsible for its welfare. (Sedna's father urges her to get married so that her husband can take care of her in the future.) Men hunted and fished while women prepared meals and looked after children. Different families came together to form communities. They helped each other survive the long winters by sharing in the hunting and fishing.

RAVEN
AND HIS
GRANDMOTHER

This myth from the
Aleut (AL ee oot) people
in Alaska reminds them that they
should be grateful for what the sea
provides and to remember to
share with their fellow villagers.

A young raven once lived with his grandmother in a barabara (bahr uh BAHR uh), a small hut made of dirt. Their home was outside the village because the villagers did not like them. The villagers lived by the sea, and the men went fishing every day. They brought home plenty of fish for their families. However, the villagers would not share with the raven and his grandmother. The raven had to hunt on his own.

This situation went on until an icy winter made fishing in the sea impossible. The villagers soon grew hungry. To take the villagers' minds off their problems, the the chief decided that his son should be married. During the celebrations, the villagers forgot their hunger. But then hunger returned.

The raven watched this from afar. All the while, he continued to hunt and bring food home to his grandmother. Then he had an idea. He visited the chief in the village and asked him a question. "If I bring you food, what will you give me in exchange?" The chief was relieved that the people would get food. He said that the raven could marry his eldest daughter in return.

The raven told his grandmother about the marriage, but she was not happy. "We have no room for a wife!" she cried. Still, the raven flew far out to sea, where he found some open water and caught some fish. He carried his prize to the chief. Then he carried the chief's daughter home as his bride. But the raven stank of fish, and the young woman could not bear to be near him. After a few days, she could stand it no more. She fled to her father's house.

The raven was not pleased, but he set his sights on another young woman.

This young woman was so hungry that she agreed to marry the raven in exchange for food. After the first night, the raven's wife could not bear the raven's smell. However, she knew that she would go hungry if she left him. Unhappily, the young woman decided to stay with the raven until the spring.

The raven was pleased. He told his grandmother to look after his wife while he went hunting. "I am going to get a large whale," said the raven. His grandmother was doubtful, but she obeyed her grandson. The next day, the raven returned with a huge whale in his mouth. The raven dropped the whale on the beach. Proudly, he told his grandmother to go and tell the villagers of his great achievement.

The hungry villagers rushed to the beach. They ate and ate. When the chief and his daughter, the raven's first wife, came to the beach, the raven would not let them feast. The chief's daughter tried to change his mind by showing the raven that he had a son. So the raven told her she could eat. But as she approached the raven, the chief's daughter realized that his fishy smell was still too much to bear. She left the beach without eating anything. The villagers later shared their food with her and the chief.

But the feasting did not save the villagers. They were so greedy that they ate too much whale fat. They also carried away a great deal of the food from the beach to store in their homes. Eventually they all died from overeating. Only three survived—the raven, his new wife, and the grandmother. They continued to live on, thanks to the generosity of the sea, which they never took for granted.

The World of THE ALEUTS

The Aleuts (AL ee ootz or uh LOOTZ) traditionally lived on the harsh, windswept Aleutian Islands, which lie off the mainland of Alaska, the state in the United States that lies along the northwestern edge of Canada. The Aleuts call themselves *Unangan* (oo NUNG eh), meaning *we the people.* They descended from Inuit (formerly called Eskimos) who settled on the islands thousands of years ago. But the Aleut language differs from that of the Inuit. There are about 12,000 Aleuts in Alaska. They follow a modern way of life, but many still hunt and fish for food.

Native Aleut women weave traditional baskets from dried grass.

ISLAND LIFE

As in "Raven and His Grandmother," the early Aleuts lived off the abundance of animals living in the waters surrounding their islands. Aleut hunters harpooned whales, seals, and other sea mammals from seagoing kayaks. They also caught fish with spears and hunted birds and moose. The islanders frequently gathered for large celebrations, such as the wedding of the chief's son described in the myth. People came together to dance, sing, feast, and tell stories.

The Aleutian (uh LOO shuhn) Islands form an archipelago, a chain of islands, in the North Pacific Ocean. More than 200 islands in the archipelago stretch in groups over 1,550 miles (2,500 km) starting from the western tip of the Alaska Peninsula. The archipelago includes over 45 volcanoes and is part of the Ring of Fire, a roughly circular chain of volcanoes around the rim of the Pacific Ocean.

RAVEN, THE TRICKSTER

A raven is a type of large, all-black bird that resembles a crow. The raven is one of the first birds mentioned in mythology. In North American myths, the raven is often a trickster, as he is in "Raven and His Grandmother." In Norse mythology, the god Odin had two sacred ravens that flew about the world each day and returned at evening to tell Odin all they had seen.

Strips of salmon dry on racks in a traditional Aleut village in Alaska in 1889.

The Aleuts traditionally lived in barabaras (left), large homes sunk 3 to 4 feet (91 to 122 centimeters) into the ground. Several Aleut families lived in a barabara. The dwelling's frame was made with drift logs or whale bones. Then the dwelling was covered with a layer of dry grass or skins and a layer of sod. Being partly buried in the soil helped to keep the barabaras warm in winter and cool in summer.

GIRL IN THE SKY

The Arapaho (uh RAP uh hoh) of the Great Plains told this story to warn people not to try to act as though they were as powerful as the gods.

A beautiful young woman called Sapana lived in a village with her family. Sapana loved watching birds of prey swoop through the sky.

One day, Sapana was gathering wood when she spotted a porcupine by a cottonwood tree. Sapana ran toward the porcupine to catch it, so she could collect its quills to make beautiful objects. The porcupine ran up the tree, so Sapana climbed after it. The porcupine climbed higher and higher, with Sapana right behind him.

When they reached the sky, the porcupine stopped. Before Sapana's eyes, the porcupine turned into an old man. He told her that she would be his wife and stay with him in the Sky World. Sapana had no choice because she had climbed too far to get back to Earth. Right away, the old man put Sapana to work. Each day, he brought her many buffalo hides. Sapana scraped and stretched them and sewed them into clothes. Sapana was miserable and wanted to go home, but there was no way back.

Sometimes, Sapana pulled up wild turnips to cook for dinner. One day, she pulled on a turnip, but it would not come loose. Finally, she grabbed the plant with two hands and pulled with all her might. When the turnip came free, Sapana saw a speck of light through the hole in the soil. This gave her an idea.

All that night Sapana thought about her plan. The next day, when her husband went out hunting, Sapana tied her buffalo hides into a rope and took them to the hole. She tied one end of the rope to her digging stick and placed the stick over the hole. Then she tied the other end around her waist.

Creeping near the hole, Sapana grasped the top of the rope and started to lower herself down.

Suddenly, Sapana's husband appeared above her. "Come back or I will cut the rope!" he yelled. "I will never come back," cried Sapana. She knew she would fall, but she also knew she did not belong in the Sky World.

The porcupine man swung the rope until the hides ripped apart. Sapana tumbled down. But then a buzzard flew under her and caught her on his back. When the buzzard grew tired, an eagle took over. Other birds of prey helped carry Sapana to the top of a tree. Dizzy but happy, Sapana rushed home to her family.

All the people of her village were grateful that Sapana had returned. From then on, the hunters always left some meat on the ground for the mighty birds of prey.

The World of THE ARAPAHO

The Arapaho (uh RAP uh hoh) who told this myth of the girl in the sky lived on the Great Plains of North America. Their world was dominated by a sky that stretched from one horizon to the other. The Arapaho moved about frequently, living in cone-shaped tents called tipis and following the bison herds, their major source of food. Today, the Arapaho work in farming, ranching, and other occupations.

THE ROLE OF WOMEN

In traditional Arapaho society, men and women had fixed roles. Men went hunting for bison, and women took care of the home, the way Sapana does in the Sky World. Women were responsible for gathering fruit and roots and cooking the buffalo meat. They also made all of the clothing.

Dyed porcupine quills decorate a pair of moccasins.

PLAINS HUNTERS

The Great Plains is a vast, dry grassland in North America. It extends for about 2,500 miles (4,020 kilometers) from northern Canada into New Mexico and Texas in the United States. In the mid-1880's, about 20 million bison thundered over the western plains. The Arapaho and other Plains Indians depended upon bison flesh for food and bison hides for clothing. In the late 1800's, white American hunters slaughtered millions of bison. This killing deprived the Indians of their main source of food and almost wiped out the bison.

Arapaho women used brightly colored porcupine quills to decorate shields, robes, blankets, teepees, and moccasins. Older women directed this quillwork and taught younger women how to do it. Quillwork design had a spiritual quality: It reflected the people's rituals and ceremonies. A quill's natural color is ivory or pale yellow, but the Arapaho used plants to dye the quills red, black, blue, and yellow.

THE COMING OF

The Dakota Sioux (soo) told this myth to explain the origin of the buffalo, on which the people depended for their survival. The myth also explains the origins of the pipe-smoking ceremony.

THE BUFFALO

In a summer long ago, the people of the nation came together and camped. They sent hunters to find game, but the men came back with nothing. Soon the people became weak with hunger.

A chief, feeling sorry for the people, decided to send his two sons out hunting. Early in the morning, the two young men left the camp. In the distance, the brothers saw a hill. They decided to climb it so they could see farther across the land. As they climbed, they saw a figure. As the figure came closer, they saw that it was a beautiful young woman. She was dressed in white buckskin that was embroidered with quills.

One of the young men could not resist her beauty. He reached out to touch the woman. Immediately, lightning struck him, and he burned up. The woman then spoke to his brother. She was Ptesan-Wi (puh tay sahn ween), White Buffalo Woman. She said she was a messenger from Wakan'tanka (wah kahn tahn kah), the Great Mystery, the creator of all things.

White Buffalo Woman told the young man to return to his camp and get the people to construct a medicine lodge for her. The young man did as she asked and told the chiefs and the people what they must do. The people made the sacred building as White Buffalo Woman instructed and waited for her arrival.

White Buffalo Woman arrived four days later. The chiefs welcomed her and listened as she explained that she wanted the people to build an altar from red soil. She told them the altar must have a rack for the holy thing she would show them.

When this was done, White Buffalo Woman showed the people her holy object—a sacred pipe. She held the stem with her right hand and the bowl with her left. She showed the people how to use the bowl. First, she filled it with tobacco. Then she walked around the lodge four times. This symbolized the circle of life. Next, she lit a fire and used the flames to light the pipe. This was the fire without end, and it would pass from one generation of the people to the next.

White Buffalo Woman showed the people how to pray and how to sing the pipe-filling song. She told them to raise the pipe up toward the sky, down toward Earth, and to the four directions of the universe. The bodies of the people, she explained, linked the sky, Earth, and all living things. The pipe, she said, holds everything and everyone together as one family.

Before she left, White Buffalo Woman told the chiefs that they must respect the pipe and its ceremony. As the people watched, she walked away. But then she stopped and rolled on the ground four times. The first time, she became a black buffalo. The second time, she turned into a brown buffalo. The third time, she became a red buffalo. At last, she rolled a fourth time. She turned into a white buffalo calf and disappeared from view.

After White Buffalo Woman left, herds of buffalo appeared on the land. The people knew to respect the buffalo and all that it gave them. It gave them meat so they would not go hungry. It gave them skins for their clothes and shelter so they would not suffer from the cold. And it gave them bones for their tools.

The World of THE DAKOTA SIOUX

The Sioux (soo) Indians traditionally lived in what is now the state of Minnesota in the upper Midwestern United States. The Sioux were famous for their bravery, fighting ability, and political skills. The Sioux had many divisions. The Santee, or Dakota, Sioux lived in what is now Minnesota. The Yankton, or Nakota, Sioux lived in the eastern Dakotas. Both of these groups hunted and farmed. The Lakota, or Teton, Sioux hunted buffalo in what are now the states of North and South Dakota and Nebraska in the upper Midwestern United States.

SMOKING THE PIPE

The Sioux and other Plains people held pipe ceremonies, as White Buffalo Woman showed them. The pipe was a symbol of protection and guidance. The people crafted pipes from wood or stone. They filled the pipe bowl with tobacco. After lighting the pipe, people said a prayer to each of the four directions and to Earth and sky.

Strips of fresh buffalo, the Indians' main food, dry in the sun to make jerky. Native Americans also roasted buffalo meat over a fire or pounded dried meat with berries and *suet* (hard animal fat) to make pemmican. The preserved meat lasted much longer than fresh meat.

A Dakota Sioux warrior wears a buffalo skin while performing a war dance. The Sioux usually danced for up to four days before setting off to raid their neighbors or to fight European Americans.

BUFFALO HUNT

The Plains Indians hunted the buffalo with bows, arrows, and spears from horseback. Sometimes the hunters worked together to drive the animals over a cliff so that they would fall and die. This was called a buffalo jump.

The arrival of the horse in North America, brought by the Spaniards in the 1600's, changed life on the Great Plains. Buffalo were difficult to hunt on foot, but on horseback the Indians could follow the buffalo herds. Buffalo hunts took place in the summer, after the Indians planted their crops.

OLD MAN COYOTE

This myth explains how the Crow people, who lived along the Yellowstone River, were created and why people were divided into different groups who often fought one another.

Back in the time when the world was still water, Old Man Coyote felt lonely. He was tired of this cold, wet world. One day, he was wandering around when he met some ducks. Old Man Coyote asked one of the ducks to dive into the water.

He wanted the duck to bring back some mud. The duck dived down. He was gone for a long time. But when the duck returned to the surface, he had no mud. Old Man Coyote asked the next duck to try. This time, the duck was under the

water for so long that Old Man Coyote worried that it would not survive. Just as he was about to give up hope, the duck's head appeared. Tired and gasping for air, the duck showed Old Man Coyote his webbed foot. Old Man Coyote was pleased. On the foot was a tiny piece of mud.

Old Man Coyote scraped the mud from the duck's foot. He started to spread the mud over the water world. Land began to form. Old Man Coyote moved west with the sun. As he traveled, he created plains, hills, and mountains. Then he created the trees and plants. Next, Old Man Coyote made all the animals that live on the land. Still, he was not finished with his creation.

Old Man Coyote decided to create people. To do this, he took some mud and rolled it into a pleasing shape. He baked the shape, and this was man. Old Man Coyote knew what it was like to be lonely, and he did not want man to be alone, so next he made woman out of mud. Old Man Coyote was pleased with his creations.

From the first man and woman, the people grew in number. Old Man

Coyote taught them music. He showed them how to perform the sun dance to honor the Creator. He told them to honor Earth, which provides for them. The people were happy, and they lived as Old Man Coyote taught them.

Because his important work was done, Old Man Coyote left Earth for a while. After a time, he returned—but he was shocked at what he found. The people, who had been happy before, were fighting with one another. Old Man Coyote shook his head. If the people could not live together, they must separate into groups. Each group would have its own mothers and its own children. In this way, Old Man Coyote divided the people into different tribes.

The World of THE CROW PEOPLE

The Crow have lived on the Yellowstone River in what are now the states of Wyoming, Montana, and North Dakota, in the upper and western Plains of the United States, for at least 300 years. The Crow were originally farmers. They were once part of another Plains tribe, the Hidatsa (hih DAHT sah), along the Missouri River in what is now North Dakota.

WHERE MUSIC BEGAN

Most native peoples believed that music originally came from the spirits. In myth, the wind brought music to the silent world. It whistled through the trees and caused the water to sing. The wind carried music to all four corners of the world. Soon, all the people could sing and make music.

The sound of beating drums is common in Native American music. The drum beat symbolizes the heartbeat of Earth. Artisans made large drums of wood and animal hides. Many groups of Indians also played wooden rattles, clappers, and flutes. Singing is as important as the drums. The songs told stories and spoke to the spirits.

Young Crow dancers take part in a dance at a powwow in Montana. The dances are seen as having a spiritual meaning for the people who take part.

The Crow could be fierce warriors. This portrait of "He Who Ties Hair Before" was painted by the American artist George Catlin in the 1800's.

DANCE

The sun dance that the Crow people learned from Old Man Coyote is one of the most important religious ceremonies of nearly all the Indian tribes of the Great Plains. It was originally performed to give thanks to the Supreme Being, represented by the sun. The Indians also used the dance to ask the Supreme Being to provide for their needs during the coming year. Today, the ceremony has different meanings for each tribe. The Indians also performed the sun dance to fulfill a vow made to a divine spirit in return for special aid. Some men tortured themselves as part of this ceremony. A sun dance lasted several days.

FATHER OF CORN

This Chippewa (CHIP uh wah) myth explains the origin of corn. It tells how a messenger from the Great Spirit was prepared to sacrifice himself to provide food for the people.

Long ago, a kind man lived with his family in a lodge. Although the man was poor, he always gave thanks to the Great Spirit for the little he had. His eldest son was kind and thoughtful like his father.

When the spring came, it was time for the young man to begin his quest. This is something all young men must do. They go out into the world to learn their spirit name and discover their purpose.

First, the young man made a hut. Then he began a fast that was to last for seven days. During this time, the young man studied the trees and plants. All the time, he wished for some way to help his people. If only he had more food, he could make them stronger! Then they would not have to spend so much time hunting and fishing. At night, the young man dreamt about these things. One night, a stranger appeared. He was dressed in robes of green and yellow.

54

I am your Guardian Spirit," said the stranger. "The Great Spirit has sent me here because he has heard your wish. From now on, your spirit name shall be Wunzh. But before I tell you how you will achieve your purpose, you must accept this challenge: You must wrestle with me three times."

By now, Wunzh was exhausted from hunger, but he was determined to honor the Great Spirit. For two nights, Wunzh and the stranger wrestled. Each time, the stranger stopped just as Wunzh felt he could take no more. On the third night, the stranger spoke again.

The Great Spirit has granted your wish," he said. "You have proved yourself honorable. Tomorrow is your last day of fasting. Your father will bring you food, and you will become strong. Then I will come, and we will wrestle to the death. You will win the challenge. Then you must strip the clothes from my body and throw me to the ground. Prepare the ground for me by removing all the weeds and roots. Then put me in the ground and cover my body with my robes and earth. Tend to the earth over me. After a time, you will know your true quest, and you will teach the others in your tribe."

The next day, Wunzh was careful to do just as the stranger had said. His father brought food, and he became strong. Then stranger returned, and they wrestled. As the stranger had promised, Wunzh was strong enough to win the contest. He prepared the ground and buried the stranger's body just as he had been instructed.

Although Wunzh returned to his family's home, he tended the grave. Carefully, he weeded the soil and added fresh earth. In the summer, he saw green shoots appearing from the soil.

In the late summer, Wunzh asked his father to come with him to the gravesite. Tall plants with yellow hair and green leaves had grown there. Yellow fruit grew on each stalk. Wunzh told his father that the Great Spirit had granted his wish. Now the people would always have this food to eat. Wunzh explained to his father how the seeds should be planted so more corn would grow.

Afterward, Wunzh held a great feast of corn for the people. They thanked the Great Spirit for the wonderful gift that could feed so many.

The World of THE CHIPPEWA

The Chippewa (CHIP uh wah), also known as the Ojibwa (oh JIHB way), are one of the largest tribal groups in North America. They once lived in the forest country around the shores of Lake Superior. For the Chippewa, corn was a basic food that supported whole communities. Wild rice was another important crop. The Chippewa were also skilled in fishing. They gathered in summer around the falls of Sault Ste. Marie, on the St. Mary's River in south-central Ontario in Canada, to spear sturgeon.

GITCHI MANITOU

The Chippewa call their Great Spirit Gitchi Manitou (gih chee muh nih doo). In Chippewa and other Algonquian myths, Gitchi Manitou is the creator of the world and everything in it, including its animals and people. For native peoples, learning how to grow corn marked a huge change in lifestyle. They no longer had to wander in small groups, hunting for food. They could settle in larger communities in villages and cultivate crops.

American Indians living in what is now Mexico learned how to grow corn (also called maize) thousands of years ago. Thus, corn came to be called Indian corn. But today the term generally refers only to varieties of corn that produce ears with multicolored kernels. Corn was eaten at most meals. Women used *cornmeal* (ground corn) to make bread. Because it was so important, corn featured in many myths.

Visions and dreams were important to many native peoples. These small webs, called dreamcatchers, were made from nets and feathers and used to prevent bad dreams.

VISION QUEST

The quest that the young man undertakes in the myth was common to many Native Americans. As part of entering manhood, an older boy spent days on his own, either in a small hut or in a remote place. In some tribes, the boy fasted for days to encourage him to start seeing visions. In other bands, the boy ate special plants that would cause visions. The people believed that through these visions, the spirits would reveal the special knowledge the boy would need to become a man and a worthy member of the people.

Chippewa men dance with other native peoples at a powwow held in honor of Earth.

DEITIES OF CANADA AND NORTHERN UNITED STATES

Coyote

Coyote appears in the myths of many North American peoples, particularly in the southwest where wild coyotes were common. Coyote is a trickster god, who sometimes helps people but sometimes causes harm and destruction. It is often difficult to know why Coyote acts in a particular way. Native peoples believed that Coyote's mischievous behavior is one of the reasons for the troubles and problems that occur in everyday life.

Great Spirit

This is another name for Wakan'tanka (wah kahn tahn kah), or the Great Mystery, of the Sioux (soo) and other peoples. The Blackfoot refer to the Great Spirit as "Old Man."

Kwatee (KWAHT ee)

For the peoples who lived around Puget Sound in what is now Washington State, in the northwestern United States, Kwatee was a trickster god whose actions were often unpredictable. His name means "the man-who-changed-things" and he helped transform the ancient world into the world as it is today. When he had completed his work, Kwatee turned himself into stone.

Ptesan-Wi (puh tay sahn ween) (White Buffalo Woman)

For the Lakota, White Buffalo Woman was a supernatural messenger on behalf of Wakan'tanka, the Great Mystery. She appeared on Earth to show the Lakota how to perform their most sacred rituals.

Raven

For the Aleut (AL ee oot), Raven was a creator god and a trickster, but he appears in the myths of many peoples, often with other names. In many myths, Raven is the victim of tricks played by Coyote.

Sedna (SEHD nuh)

The Inuit believed that Sedna was the goddess of the sea. She helped humans by providing food, but she was also sinister and angry, and her outbursts of temper caused violent storms. Sedna lives beneath the sea, where she rules the dead who disobeyed her wishes in life.

Sky Woman

In Haudenosaunee (hoe dee noh SHOH nee), or Iroquois, myth, Sky Woman was the grandmother of the creator twins, Tsentsa and Taweskare. During one of twins' fights, Sky Woman was killed. They threw her head into the sky, where it became the moon.

Taweskare (tah weh skah reh)

To the Haudenosaunee, Taweskare or Tawiscara was the spirit of evil. He and his twin brother, Tsentsa, were the grandsons of Sky Woman. Taweskare was evil and harmful but Tsentsa was good and protective. The twins battled to gain domination over the world. Their battle ended in Taweskare being banished to the west.

Thunderbird

Native peoples from the Pacific Northwest to the southeast believed in a form of the Thunderbird. This creature had huge wings that caused thunder when they flapped. Some peoples believed that it could make lightning with its eyes and cause rain to fall.

Tsentsa

For the Haudenosaunee, Tsentsa—sometimes also called Ioskeha—was the god of everything that was good in the world. He and his twin brother, the evil Taweskare, battled to gain domination over the world.

Wakan'tanka (wah kahn tahn kah) (Great Mystery)

Among the Sioux, Wakan'tanka was the Great Mystery who created the universe and was the provider of all the benefits enjoyed by humans.

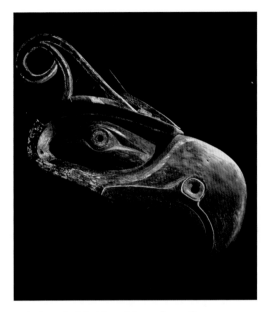

A thunderbird headdress from the Kwakiutl (kwah kee OO tuhl) culture in the Pacific Northwest would have been worn by a dancer performing a sacred dance.

GLOSSARY

confederation An alliance of peoples that act together for the good of everyone.

creation The process by which the universe was brought into being at the start of time.

creator In myth, a creator god is one that creates the universe or the earth, geographical features, and often all humans or a particular culture. Creation myths explain the origins of the world, but often do so by describing actions that seem to take place in a world that already exists.

First Nations The aboriginal Indian peoples of Canada; sometimes also used to describe indigenous peoples of North America.

glacier A slowly moving sheet of ice formed by a thick layer of compacted snow sliding over the land.

igloo A dome-shaped structure built by the Inuit from blocks of solid snow and used as homes or as temporary shelters.

kayak A type of canoe used by the Inuit, which has a wooden frame with a waterproof covering.

moccasin A soft leather shoe or slipper in which a single sole is folded up and sewed to an upper, leaving a hole for the foot.

myth A traditional story that a people tell to explain their origins or the origins of natural and social phenomena. Myths often involve gods, spirits, and supernatural beings.

quillwork A type of decoration created by various peoples, who dyed and softened porcupine quills to make elaborate designs.

ritual A religious ceremony in which a set of actions are peformed in a specific order.

sacred Something that is connected with the gods or goddesses and so should be treated with respectful worship.

sacrifice An offering made to a god or gods, often in the form of an animal or even a person who is killed for the purpose. Sacrifices also take the shape of valued possessions that might be buried, placed in caves, or thrown into a lake for the gods.

supernatural Describes something that cannot be explained by science or by the laws of nature, which is therefore said to be caused by beings such as gods, spirits, or ghosts.

symbolize To represent something else. Symbols often take the form of physical objects or signs that represent abstract qualities.

tipi A conical tent used by peoples who lived on the plains and around the Great Lakes. The tipi is made from wooden poles covered with animal skins or canvas, and it can easily be taken down and moved to a new location.

trickster A supernatural figure who engages in many mischievous activities that sometimes benefit and sometimes harm humans. The motives behind a trickster's behavior are not always clear. Tricksters appear in various shapes in myths around the world, including Coyote and Raven in Native American cultures and Anansi the spider in West Africa.

vision The experience of seeing someone or something in a dream or a trance, which can be encouraged by consuming certain foods or drinks. Native Americans believe that supernatural spirits appear in visions to pass their wisdom to humans.

FOR FURTHER INFORMATION

Books

Bruchac, James, and Joseph Bruchac. *The Girl Who Helped Thunder and Other Native American Folktales* (Folktales of the World). Sterling, 2008.

Dalal, Anita. *Native American Myths* (Myths from Around the World). Gareth Stevens Publishing, 2010.

Dembicki, Matt. *Trickster: Native American Tales: A Graphic Collection.* Fulcrum Books, 2010.

Edmonds, Margot, and Ella E. Clark. *Voices of the Winds: Native American Legends.* Castle Books, 2003.

Jones, David, and Brian L. Molyneaux. *The Illustrated Encyclopedia of American Indian Mythology: Legends, Gods, and Spirits of North, Central, and South America.* Anness, 2010.

Kaslik, Ibi. *Tales from the Tundra: A Collection of Inuit Stories.* Inhabit Media, 2010.

Kopp, Megan. *Understanding Native American Myths* (Myths Understood). Crabtree Publishing, 2013.

Mathis, Andy, and Marian Wood. *Native American Civilizations* (Ancient Civilizations and their Myths and Legends). Rosen Central, 2010.

Morris, Neil. *Native American Myths* (Myths from Many Lands). Skyview Books, 2009.

National Geographic Essential Visual History of World Mythology. National Geographic Society, 2008.

Philip, Neil. *Eyewitness Mythology* (DK Eyewitness Books). DK Publishing, 2011.

Pomplun, Tom, ed. *American Classics.* Eureka Productions, 2013

Schomp, Virginia. *The Native Americans* (Myths of the World). Marshall Cavendish Benchmark, 2008.

Wolfson, Evelyn. *Mythology of the American Indians* (Mythology, Myths, and Legends). Enslow Publishers, 2015.

Zimmerman, Larry J. *Exploring the Life, Myth, and Art of Native Americans* (Civilizations of the World). Rosen Publishing Group, 2010.

Websites

http://americanfolklore.net/folklore/native-american-myths/
Retellings of famous myths from Native American and First Nation peoples.

http://www.native-languages.org/legends.htm
Index of Native American myths, listed by tribe, with links to thematic indexes.

http://www.crystalinks.com/nativeamcreation.html
A collection of creation myths from various Native American tribes.

http://www.indigenouspeople.net/stories.htm
Library of online myths and legends, with regional collections of stories and a section of stories about different animals.

http://www.thecanadianencyclopedia.ca/en/article/inuit-myth-and-legend/
Article from the *Canadian Encyclopedia* about Inuit myth.

http://www.sacred-texts.com/nam/sioux.htm
Retellings of many myths and legends of the Sioux.

INDEX

PRONUNCIATION KEY

Sound	As in
a	hat, map
ah	father, far
ai	care, air
aw	order
aw	all
ay	age, face
ch	child, much
ee	equal, see
ee	machine, city
eh	let, best
ih	it, pin, hymn
k	coat, look
o	hot, rock
oh	open, go
oh	grow, tableau
oo	rule, move, food
ow	house, out
oy	oil, voice
s	say, nice
sh	she, abolition
u	full, put
u	wood
uh	cup, butter
uh	flood
uh	about, ameba
uh	taken, purple
uh	pencil
uh	lemon
uh	circus
uh	labyrinth
uh	curtain
uh	Egyptian
uh	section
uh	fabulous
ur	term, learn, sir, work
y	icon, ice, five
yoo	music
zh	pleasure